OMAD COOKBOOK

MEGA BUNDLE – 4 Manuscripts in 1 – 160+ OMAD- friendly recipes including pie, cookie, and smoothies for a delicious and tasty diet

TABLE OF CONTENTS

Introduction

OMAD recipes for personal enjoyment but also for family enjoyment. You will love them for sure for how easy it is to prepare them.

BREAKFAST

CHICKEN EGG ROLL

Serves: **4**

Prep Time: **10**   Minutes

Cook Time: **10**   Minutes

Total Time: **20**   Minutes

INGREDIENTS

- 3 ½ ounces chicken breast
- 1 dash salt
- ½ packages stevia
- 3 cabbage leaves
- 1 cup shredded cabbage
- 2 Melba toast

DIRECTIONS

1. Steam the cabbage leaves for 5 minutes.
2. Add the shredded cabbage and steam for 5 minutes.
3. Place the cabbage in a bowl along with the chicken and the spices.
4. Wrap the mixture in cabbage leaves and serve topped with Melba toast.

Serves: **12**

Prep Time: **10** Minutes

Cook Time: **30** Minutes

Total Time: **40** Minutes

INGREDIENTS

- 1 cup cheese
- 8 eggs
- ¼ cup water
- 1 handful spinach
- 10 slices bacon
- ½ tbs Dijon mustard
- 1 tsp hot sauce
- Salt
- Pepper

DIRECTIONS

1. Preheat the oven to 350F.
2. Divide the spinach, cheese, and bacon into 12 greased cups of a cupcake tin.
3. Whisk together the water, eggs, mustard, hot sauce, salt, and pepper in a bowl.
4. Fill the cups with the egg mixture within 1/4 -inch from top.

5. Stir each cup, then bake for 30 minutes.
6. Serve hot.

EGG BAKE

Serves: **4**

Prep Time: **10** Minutes

Cook Time: **40** Minutes

Total Time: **50** Minutes

INGREDIENTS

- 4 eggs
- ¾ cup cheese
- ½ rice avocado
- Sour cream
- ½ onion
- 6 bacon strips
- 1 can diced tomatoes
- ½ tsp cayenne pepper
- 4 egg whites
- Hot sauce
- ½ red bell pepper
- ½ green bell pepper

DIRECTIONS

1. Whisk the eggs with the egg whites and cayenne pepper in a bowl.
2. Saute the onions, peppers and bacon until cooked.

3. Mix the tomatoes, cheese, egg and pepper mixture together in a baking dish.
4. Bake for 40 minutes.
5. Serve topped with avocado, sour cream and hot sauce.

BREAKFAST CASSEROLE

Serves: **4**

Prep Time: **10**   Minutes

Cook Time: **40**   Minutes

Total Time: **50**   Minutes

INGREDIENTS

- 2 poblano chile peppers
- 12 ounces chicken sausage
- ½ tsp garlic powder
- ½ tsp onion powder
- ½ tsp salt
- 2 garlic cloves
- 12 egg whites
- 4 eggs
- 1 cup milk
- 2 tbs cilantro
- ½ tsp black pepper
- ¼ cup green onion
- 1 tsp olive oil
- ½ onion
- 4 oz. cheddar cheese
- Oil
- Sour cream

- 1 tsp hot sauce
- ½ tsp chili powder
- ½ red bell pepper

DIRECTIONS

1. Preheat the oven to 350F.
2. Roast the poblanos.
3. Place the peppers aside until cool enough to handle.
4. Peel the skin off and remove the seeds and stems.
5. Place the peppers in a greased baking dish.
6. Cook the chicken sausage until brown.
7. Remove from heat and spoon over the peppers.
8. Saute the onion and bell peppers in the oil.
9. Add the garlic and stir for a minute.
10. Spoon the mixture over the poblanos.
11. Top with the green onions and cilantro.
12. Whisk the eggs, egg whites, chili powder, onion powder, hot sauce, garlic powder, milk, salt, and pepper in a bowl.
13. Pour into baking dish, coating all of the ingredients.
14. Add cheese on top.
15. Bake for 30 minutes, remove and serve

SCOTCH EGGS

Serves: **6**

Prep Time: **10** Minutes

Cook Time: **40** Minutes

Total Time: **50** Minutes

INGREDIENTS

- 1 lb breakfast sausage
- 6 hard-boiled eggs
- ¼ cup flour
- 1 egg
- 1 ½ cups panko bread crumbs
- 4 tbs oil

DIRECTIONS

1. Preheat the oven to 350F.
2. Divide the sausage into 6 portions.
3. Wrap the eggs with the sausage.
4. Roll them into flour, egg wash, and panko crumbs in this order.
5. Preheat the oil in a pan.
6. Cook the balls until brown on all sides.
7. Place on a tray.
8. Bake for 25 minutes, remove and serve

SUNNY-SIDE UP EGG

Serves: *4*
Prep Time: *10*   Minutes

Cook Time: *10*   Minutes

Total Time: *20*   Minutes

INGREDIENTS

- 1 egg
- 6 tbs egg whites
- ¼ spinach
- 3 tbs green onion
- Salt
- Pepper

DIRECTIONS

1. Preheat the burner.
2. Grease a skillet with cooking spray.
3. Crack the egg into the skillet and add 6 tbs egg whites.

EGG WHITE TOSTADA

Serves: *1*

Prep Time: *5*   Minutes

Cook Time: *5*   Minutes

Total Time: *10* Minutes

INGREDIENTS

- 2 toast
- ½ tsp cilantro
- Pepper
- 1 egg white
- 1 tsp salsa
- 2 tbs water
- Salt

DIRECTIONS

1. Cook the egg white in a pan, then season with salt and pepper and add 1 tbs water.
2. Cook for ½ minute covered.
3. Divide in 2 and place each half on the toast.
4. Top with salsa and cilantro.

Serves: *1*

Prep Time: *5*   Minutes

Cook Time: *5*   Minutes

Total Time: *10*   Minutes

INGREDIENTS

- 5 tbs salsa
- 1 egg
- 5 tbs egg substitute
- Salt
- Pepper

DIRECTIONS

1. Scramble the eggs.
2. Add the egg substitute and cook.
3. Season with salt and pepper.
4. Serve topped with salsa.

BREAKFAST PIZZA

Serves: **2**

Prep Time: **5** Minutes

Cook Time: **10** Minutes

Total Time: **15** Minutes

INGREDIENTS

- 1 egg
- 2 egg whites
- Cheese
- Salt
- Red pepper
- Tomatoes
- Milk
- Mushrooms
- Pepper
- Green pepper

DIRECTIONS

1. Whisk the eggs, egg whites, and milk together.
2. Cook in a skillet for 3 minutes.
3. When almost set, top with the vegetables and add cheese on top.
4. Serve immediately.

FRENCH TOAST

Serves: **4**

Prep Time: **10** Minutes

Cook Time: **10** Minutes

Total Time: **20** Minutes

INGREDIENTS

- Bread slices
- Egg substitute
- 1 tsp cinnamon
- Stevia
- 1 tsp vanilla
- Butter

DIRECTIONS

1. Mix the egg substitute, vanilla, and cinnamon in a bowl.
2. Melt the butter in a skillet.
3. Coat the bread slices with the egg mixture.
4. Cook until golden.
5. Serve immediately.

SPANICH OMELET

Serves: **2**

Prep Time: **10**   Minutes

Cook Time: **10**   Minutes

Total Time: **20**   Minutes

INGREDIENTS

- 6 eggs
- 1 ½ cups bell peppers
- 1 onion
- Salt
- Pepper
- Thyme
- 1 can potatoes

DIRECTIONS

1. Whisk the eggs together in a bowl.
2. Season and add the vegetables.
3. Cook until fluffy.
4. Serve hot.

APPLE CRUMB CAKE

Serves: **4**

Prep Time: **10**   Minutes

Cook Time: **30**   Minutes

Total Time: **40**   Minutes

INGREDIENTS
Cake
- 1 egg
- 1 cup flour
- 1 tsp baking soda
- ½ cup yogurt
- ½ cup apple sauce
- 1 cup brown sugar
- 1 tsp vanilla
- 1 ½ cups apple cored

Topping
- 3 tbs brown sugar
- 3 tbs flour
- 1 tbs butter

DIRECTIONS

1. Mix all of the cake ingredients in a bowl.
2. Place on a baking sheet.
3. Mix the topping ingredients, then add over the cake.

4. Bake for 30 minutes.

5. Allow to cool, then serve.

BREAKFAST QUINOA

Serves: **2**

Prep Time: **10** Minutes

Cook Time: **20** Minutes

Total Time: **30** Minutes

INGREDIENTS

- 2 tbs water
- 1 tbs brown sugar
- ¼ cup coconut flakes
- 1 cup bananas
- ½ cup quinoa
- ¾ cup coconut milk
- 1 cup strawberries

DIRECTIONS

1. Cook the quinoa.
2. When half done, add the coconut milk and sugar and mix well.
3. Cook until done.
4. Toast the coconut flakes.
5. Serve topped with fruits and flakes.

BREAKFAST TACOS

Serves: **2**

Prep Time: **10** Minutes

Cook Time: **10** Minutes

Total Time: **20** Minutes

INGREDIENTS

- 2 tortillas
- 2 cups spinach leaves
- 4 eggs
- Oil
- 1 tsp cumin
- Cilantro
- Hot sauce
- 1 tsp turmeric
- ½ cup beans
- Salt
- Pepper

DIRECTIONS

1. Cook the beans with the hot sauce and spices.
2. Garnish with cilantro.
3. Fry the spinach leaves.

4. Scramble the eggs.
5. Add the beans, eggs and spinach leaves on the tortillas.
6. Serve topped with avocado slices and garnished with cilantro.

BLUEBERRY OATS

Serves: **2**
Prep Time: **5** Minutes

Cook Time: **10** Minutes

Total Time: **15** Minutes

INGREDIENTS

- 2 cups blueberries
- 1 tsp lemon rind
- 1 tbs lemon juice
- 1 cup oats
- ¼ cup brown sugar
- ½ tsp cinnamon powder
- 4 cups water
- Salt

DIRECTIONS

1. Prepare the compote.
2. Prepare the oats.
3. Serve the oats with the compote.

MUSHROOM OMELETTE

Serves: *1*
Prep Time: *5*   Minutes

Cook Time: *10* Minutes

Total Time: *15* Minutes

INGREDIENTS

- 2 eggs
- ¼ tsp salt
- ¼ tsp black pepper
- 1 tablespoon olive oil
- ¼ cup cheese
- ¼ tsp basil
- 1 cup mushrooms

DIRECTIONS

1. In a bowl combine all ingredients together and mix well
2. In a skillet heat olive oil and pour the egg mixture
3. Cook for 1-2 minutes per side
4. When ready remove omelette from the skillet and serve

OVERNIGHT OATMEAL

Serves: *8*
Prep Time: *10*   Minutes

Cook Time: *6*   Hours

Total Time: *40*   Minutes

INGREDIENTS

- 7 cups water
- 1/3 cup apricots
- 2 cups of oats
- 2/3 cup cranberries

DIRECTIONS

1. Mix the ingredients together in a slow cooker
2. Cook on low for at least 6 hours

MORNING FRITTATA

Serves: **2**

Prep Time: **10** Minutes

Cook Time: **15** Minutes

Total Time: **25** Minutes

INGREDIENTS

- 1/3 chicken broth
- 1 green onion
- 1 garlic clove
- Salt
- Pepper
- Herbs
- 2 tomatoes
- 1 ½ cups spinach
- 4 eggs
- 5 slices bacon

DIRECTIONS

1. Preheat oven to 350 F
2. Fry the bacon
3. Mix the eggs, broth and seasonings together well
4. Place the spinach at the bottom of a skillet and pour the batter over
5. Add the remaining ingredients, bake for 15 minutes

Serves: *4*
Prep Time: *10*   Minutes

Cook Time: *10*   Minutes

Total Time: *20*   Minutes

INGREDIENTS

- 2-3 tbs oil
- 1 garlic clove
- Pepper
- 1 cup green beans
- 2 lb potatoes
- Salt
- 4 eggs

DIRECTIONS

1. Peel and dice the potatoes then boil until starting to soften
2. Dice the green beans and cook for almost 5 minutes then drain
3. Cook the potatoes in hot oil until crispy then add the green beans and the garlic
4. Crack the eggs over and cook covered for at least 5 minutes
5. Season and serve

TUNA SANDWICH

Serves: **4**

Prep Time: 5   Minutes

Cook Time: 5   Minutes

Total Time: **10**   Minutes

INGREDIENTS

- Mayonnaise
- Salt
- Pepper
- Bread
- 1 tuna tin
- Celery

DIRECTIONS

1. Mix the tuna, mayonnaise and celery together then season
2. Toast the bread
3. Spread the tuna mixture over the bread and serve

ZUCCHINI BREAD

Serves: *4*
Prep Time: *10* Minutes

Cook Time: *40* Minutes

Total Time: *50* Minutes

INGREDIENTS

- 4 tbs honey
- 5 tbs oil
- 1 ½ tsp baking soda
- 3 eggs
- ½ cup walnuts
- 2 ½ cups flour
- 4 Medjool dates
- 1 banana
- 2 tsp mixed spice
- 1 ½ cup zucchini

DIRECTIONS

1. Preheat the oven to 350 F
2. Chop the dates and the walnuts
3. Mix the flour, spice and baking soda together
4. Mix the eggs and banana in a food processor then add remaining ingredients and mix

5. Pour the batter into a pan and cook for at least 40 minutes
6. Allow to cool then serve

Serves: *1*
Prep Time: *5*   Minutes

Cook Time: *5*   Minutes

Total Time: *10* Minutes

INGREDIENTS

- Porridge
- Honey
- Blueberries
- Almonds
- 1 banana
- Chia seeds

DIRECTIONS

1. Mix everything together
2. Serve drizzled with honey

PANCAKES

BANANA PANCAKES

Serves: **4**

Prep Time: **10**   Minutes

Cook Time: **20**   Minutes

Total Time: **30**   Minutes

INGREDIENTS

- 1 cup whole wheat flour
- ¼ tsp baking soda
- ¼ tsp baking powder
- 1 cup mashed banana
- 2 eggs
- 1 cup milk

DIRECTIONS

1. In a bowl combine all ingredients together and mix well
2. In a skillet heat olive oil
3. Pour ¼ of the batter and cook each pancake for 1-2 minutes per side
4. When ready remove from heat and serve

FLUFFY GREEK YOGURT PANCAKES

Serves: **4**
Prep Time: **10**   Minutes

Cook Time: **10**   Minutes

Total Time: **20**   Minutes

INGREDIENTS

- 1 egg
- 2 cups berries
- 2 tsp baking soda
- 2 cups Greek yogurt
- ½ tsp salt
- 1 tsp vanilla
- 2 ½ tbs maple syrup
- 1 ½ cup flour

DIRECTIONS

1. Mix well the ingredients in a bowl.
2. Cook the pancakes in a skillet for 3 minutes on each side.
3. Serve topped with maple syrup.

PUMPKIN PANCAKES

Serves: **7**

Prep Time: **10** Minutes

Cook Time: **10** Minutes

Total Time: **20** Minutes

INGREDIENTS

- 1 cup flour
- 1/3 cup flax seed meal
- 1/3 cup milk
- 1 ½ tbs oil
- 1 tsp lemon juice
- 2 tsp cinnamon
- 2 eggs
- ½ ts ginger
- 2 tbs honey
- ½ tsp nutmeg
- 2/3 cup pureed pumpkin
- 2/7 tsp cloves
- 1/3 tsp baking soda

DIRECTIONS

1. Mix the dry ingredients together in a bowl
2. Mix the wet ingredients together in another bowl

3. Mix the ingredients by adding the dry ingredients to the wet ones to form a batter

4. Heat the oil in a skillet and pour the batter using a small ladle

5. Fry until gold

PANCAKES

Serves: *8*
Prep Time: *10*   Minutes

Cook Time: *15*   Minutes

Total Time: *25*   Minutes

INGREDIENTS

- 1 egg
- ½ tsp vanilla
- ½ tsp baking powder
- Salt
- ½ tsp flour
- Cinnamon
- Stevia
- ½ cup water

DIRECTIONS

1. Mix all of the ingredients and form a batter.
2. Fry in coconut oil.
3. Serve with your favorite toppings.

BREAKFAST COOKIES

Serves: **8-12**

Prep Time: **5** Minutes

Cook Time: **15** Minutes

Total Time: **20** Minutes

INGREDIENTS

- 1 cup rolled oats
- ¼ cup applesauce
- ½ tsp vanilla extract
- 3 tablespoons chocolate chips
- 2 tablespoons dried fruits
- 1 tsp cinnamon

DIRECTIONS

1. Preheat the oven to 325 F
2. In a bowl combine all ingredients together and mix well
3. Scoop cookies using an ice cream scoop
4. Place cookies onto a prepared baking sheet
5. Place in the oven for 12-15 minutes or until the cookies are done
6. When ready remove from the oven and serve

BREAKFAST BISCUITS

Serves: **6**

Prep Time: **5**   Minutes

Cook Time: **15**   Minutes

Total Time: **20**   Minutes

INGREDIENTS

- 6 tbs milk
- 3 tbs water
- 3 tbs mayonnaise
- 1 cup flour

DIRECTIONS

1. Mix the ingredients except for the mayo in a bowl.
2. Add in the mayonnaise and mix.
3. Stir in the water and milk.
4. Form balls and place on a baking sheet.
5. Bake for 15 minutes.
6. Serve immediately.

SMOOTHIES

BERRY SMOOTHIE

Serves: **4**
Prep Time: **5**   Minutes

Cook Time: **5**   Minutes

Total Time: **10** Minutes

INGREDIENTS

- ½ cup strawberries
- ½ cup blueberries
- ½ cup cranberries
- ½ cup raspberries
- 1 cup milk
- 1 banana
- 3 cubes ice

DIRECTIONS

1. In a blender place all ingredients and blend until smooth
2. Pour smoothie in a glass and serve

PEACHY SMOOTHIE

Serves: 2

Prep Time: 5   Minutes

Cook Time: 5   Minutes

Total Time: *10*   Minutes

INGREDIENTS

- 1 peach
- ½ cup tofu
- 1 tablespoon sugar
- 1 cup milk
- 1 cup raspberries

DIRECTIONS

1. In a blender place all ingredients and blend until smooth
2. Pour smoothie in a glass and serve

APPLE SMOOTHIE

Serves: *1*
Prep Time: 5   Minutes

Cook Time: 5   Minutes

Total Time: *10*   Minutes

INGREDIENTS

- ½ cup banana
- ½ cup yogurt
- ½ cup applesauce
- ½ cup milk

DIRECTIONS

1. In a blender place all ingredients and blend until smooth
2. Pour smoothie in a glass and serve

CHERRY-LICIOUS SMOOTHIE

Serves: **2**

Prep Time: **5**   Minutes

Cook Time: **5**   Minutes

Total Time: **10**   Minutes

INGREDIENTS

- ½ cup cherries
- 1 apple
- ½ cup yogurt
- 1 tablespoon agave syrup
- 2 ice cubes

DIRECTIONS

1. Peel the cherries and apple and cut them into small cubes
2. In a blender place all ingredients and blend until smooth
3. Pour smoothie in a glass and serve

CARROT SMOOTHIE

Serves: **2**

Prep Time: **5**   Minutes

Cook Time: **5**   Minutes

Total Time: **10** Minutes

INGREDIENTS

- 2 apples
- 5 baby carrots
- 1 orange
- 1 cup spinach

DIRECTIONS

1. In a blender place all ingredients and blend until smooth
2. Pour smoothie in a glass and serve

PINEAPPLE SMOOTHIE

Serves: **2**

Prep Time: **5**   Minutes

Cook Time: **5**   Minutes

Total Time: **10**   Minutes

INGREDIENTS

-   1 cup pineapple
-   2 cups blueberries
-   1 tablespoon sugar
-   ½ cup water

DIRECTIONS

1. In a blender place all ingredients and blend until smooth
2. Pour smoothie in a glass and serve

PEAR SMOOTHIE

Serves: **2**

Prep Time: **5**   Minutes

Cook Time: **5**   Minutes

Total Time: **10** Minutes

INGREDIENTS

- 1 banana
- 1 pear
- 1 apple
- 1 cup yogurt
- 2 tablespoons seeds

DIRECTIONS

1. In a blender place all ingredients and blend until smooth
2. Pour smoothie in a glass and serve

MANGO SMOOTHIE

Serves: *1*

Prep Time: 5   Minutes

Cook Time: 5   Minutes

Total Time: *10*   Minutes

INGREDIENTS

- 1 cup mango
- 1 cup pineapple
- 2 cups spinach
- ½ cup water

DIRECTIONS

1. In a blender place all ingredients and blend until smooth
2. Pour smoothie in a glass and serve

MUFFINS

SIMPLE MUFFINS

Serves: *8-12*

Prep Time: *10*   Minutes

Cook Time: *20*   Minutes

Total Time: *30*   Minutes

INGREDIENTS

- 2 eggs
- 1 tablespoon olive oil
- 1 cup milk
- 2 cups whole wheat flour
- 1 tsp baking soda
- ¼ tsp baking soda
- 1 cup pumpkin puree
- 1 tsp cinnamon
- ¼ cup molasses

DIRECTIONS

1. In a bowl combine all dry ingredients
2. In another bowl combine all dry ingredients
3. Combine wet and dry ingredients together
4. Pour mixture into 8-12 prepared muffin cups, fill 2/3 of the cups

5. Bake for 18-20 minutes at 375 F
6. When ready remove from the oven and serve

CRANBERRY MUFFINS

Serves: **12**

Prep Time: **5**   Minutes

Cook Time: **25**   Minutes

Total Time: **30**   Minutes

INGREDIENTS

- 1 ½ cups flour
- 1 tsp baking soda
- 1/8 tsp cloves
- 1 cup brown sugar
- 1 cup pumpkin puree
- 1 tsp ginger
- 1/3 cup milk
- 1 egg
- 2 tbs oil
- ½ cup cranberries
- ½ tsp cinnamon
- 1/3 tsp baking powder
- Salt

DIRECTIONS

1. Pulse all of the ingredients in a food processor.

2. Pour the batter into 12 muffin cups.

3. Bake for 25 minutes.

4. Serve warm.

BANANA MUFFINS

Serves: **4**

Prep Time: **10** Minutes

Cook Time: **30** Minutes

Total Time: **40** Minutes

INGREDIENTS

- 2 cups flour
- 2 bananas
- 1 egg
- 1 tsp baking soda
- 2 tsp cinnamon
- 1 tsp baking powder
- 1/3 cup oats
- 2 tbs honey
- 1 cup milk

DIRECTIONS

1. Preheat the oven to 350 F
2. Mix well the eggs, honey, milk, and banana in a bowl
3. Separately, mix the flour, baking soda, baking powder, oats and cinnamon.
4. Combine the eggs mixture and the flour mixture together gently
5. Pour into the muffin tray and bake until golden

CARROT MUFFINS

Serves: **12**

Prep Time: **15** Minutes

Cook Time: **30** Minutes

Total Time: **45** Minutes

INGREDIENTS

- 1/3 cup flour
- 1 ½ tsp nutmeg
- ½ tp vinegar
- 4 carrots
- 3 tbs butter
- ½ tsp molasses
- 1 cup butter
- 1 egg
- 10 dates
- ¼ tsp salt
- 1 tsp baking soda
- 1 banana

DIRECTIONS

1. Preheat the oven to 350 F
2. Whisk the egg in a bowl then add 3 tb of melted butter and mix well

3. Chop the dates well to form a paste
4. Mix the date paste, mashed banana, nutmeg, molasses, and melted butter
5. Add the mixture over the egg
6. Add the flour, mix then add the baking soda and vinegar
7. Pour the batter into a lined muffin pan
8. Allow to cool then serve

EGG MUFFINS

Serves: **12**

Prep Time: **10** Minutes

Cook Time: **30** Minutes

Total Time: **40** Minutes

INGREDIENTS

- Vegetables
- Meat
- 1 ½ tsp seasoning
- 12 eggs
- 12 muffin tin liners
- 1 cup cheese

DIRECTIONS

1. Place the diced meat and vegetables and cheese in the bottom of the muffin cups.
2. Beat the eggs and season in a bowl.
3. Pour the eggs into the cups and bake for 30 minutes.
4. Serve hot.

SECOND COOKBOOK

MUSHROOM OMELETTE

Serves: **1**

Prep Time: **5**   Minutes

Cook Time: **5**   Minutes

Total Time: **10**   Minutes

INGREDIENTS

- 2 eggs
- Bacon
- 2 tsp coconut oil
- Nutmeg
- 1 red onion
- Salt
- Pepper

DIRECTIONS

1. Sauté the onion in the coconut oil for a few minutes.
2. Slice the mushrooms and add them to the pan, with salt and nutmeg.
3. Cook for another few minutes.
4. Remove the mushrooms from the pan.
5. Cook the beaten eggs for 3 minutes.

6. Serve the omelette topped with the mushroom mixture and bacon.

AVOCADO TOAST

Serves: *1*

Prep Time: *5*   Minutes

Cook Time: *10*   Minutes

Total Time: *15*   Minutes

INGREDIENTS

- 1 clove garlic
- ½ avocado
- 1 egg
- Salt
- 1 slice toast
- Pepper
- Red pepper flakes

DIRECTIONS

1. Grate ½ clove of garlic into a pan, add the egg on top and cook to the desired degree of doneness.
2. Toast the bread.
3. Smash the avocado with a fork.
4. Spread the avocado over the toast.
5. Top with the fried egg and garlic, season, and serve.

TOMATO SHAKSHUKA

Serves: *4*

Prep Time: *10* Minutes

Cook Time: *50* Minutes

Total Time: *60* Minutes

INGREDIENTS

- 1 pinch cayenne
- Salt
- 1 red bell pepper
- 4 eggs
- ¼ cup olive oil
- 1 tbs cumin seeds
- 1 yellow onion
- 2 thyme sprigs
- 1 tbs parsley
- 1 ½ lb cherry tomatoes

DIRECTIONS

1. Preheat the oven to 350F.
2. Cut the tomatoes and place them on a cookie sheet, then season with salt.
3. Bake until fully roasted.
4. Roast the cumin seeds for 1 minute.

5. Add the olive oil and onion and saute until soft.

6. Add the strips chopped pepper, chopped herbs, and tomatoes.

7. Add the salt and cayenne pepper.

8. Pour the eggs into the pan and cook on low until the egg white is set.

9. Serve immediately.

PORTOBELLO MUSHROOM CAPS

Serves: *1*

Prep Time: 5   Minutes

Cook Time: 5   Minutes

Total Time: *10*   Minutes

INGREDIENTS

- 50g ham
- Salt
- Pepper
- ¼ cup watercress
- 1 Portobello mushroom
- 1 poached egg
- ½ avocado

DIRECTIONS

1. Cook the mushrooms in coconut oil for 1 minute per side.
2. Season with salt and set aside.
3. Poach the eggs.
4. Pot each Portobello cap with the sliced avocado, a handful of watercress leaves, and ham.
5. Place the egg over, sprinkle with salt and pepper and serve.

EGG IN AVOCADO

Serves: **2**

Prep Time: **5**   Minutes

Cook Time: **10** Minutes

Total Time: **15** Minutes

INGREDIENTS

- 1 avocado
- 2 eggs
- Cheese
- Salt
- Pepper

DIRECTIONS

1. Preheat the oven to 425F.
2. Slice the avocado in half and remove the pit.
3. Crave out a little space in the center and crack the egg there.
4. Top with cheese.
5. Cook until the cheese is melted and the egg is done.
6. Serve immediately.

OMELETTE BITES

Serves: *12*

Prep Time: *5*   Minutes

Cook Time: *35*   Minutes

Total Time: *40*   Minutes

INGREDIENTS

- 4 eggs
- 1 green pepper
- 2 cups diced cooked chicken
- 2 cups spinach
- 1 avocado
- 12 egg whites
- Pepper
- 12 slices bacon
- 1 red pepper

DIRECTIONS

1. Preheat the oven to 350F.
2. Cook the bacon for 5 minutes, making sure it's not crispy.
3. Grease a muffin tin and place one piece of bacon in each tin, wrapping it around the outer edges.
4. Whisk together in a bowl the eggs, egg whites, salt, pepper, peppers, chicken, and spinach.

5. Mix well then pour into each muffin tin.
6. Bake for 30 minutes, serve topped with avocado.

MACADAMIA WAFFLES

Serves: **6**

Prep Time: **10** Minutes

Cook Time: **3** Minutes

Total Time: **40** Minutes

INGREDIENTS

- 4 tbs coconut flour
- 1 cup macadamia nuts
- ½ cup coconut milk
- 1 tsp baking powder
- 3 eggs
- 1 tsp vanilla
- 3 tbs maple syrup
- 3 tbs coconut oil

DIRECTIONS

1. Preheat the waffle iron.
2. Blend all of the ingredients for 30 seconds on low.
3. Blend on high for another 30 seconds, until completely smooth.
4. Pour the batter into the waffle iron.
5. Cook on low for 50 seconds.
6. Serve topped with your desired syrups.

BACON & AVOCADO SANDWICHES

Serves: **2**

Prep Time: **5**   Minutes

Cook Time: **5**   Minutes

Total Time: **10**   Minutes

INGREDIENTS

- Salt
- 1 avocado
- 4 strips bacon
- 1 lime

DIRECTIONS

1. Cook the bacon.
2. Mash the avocado with lime juice and salt.
3. Place the avocado mixture between the bacon slices.
4. Serve immediately.

ZUCCHINI FRITTATA

Serves: *4*
Prep Time: *10* Minutes

Cook Time: *25* Minutes

Total Time: *35* Minutes

INGREDIENTS

- 1 sweet potato
- 2 zucchinis
- 8 eggs
- 1 red bell pepper
- 2 tbs coconut oil
- 2 tbs parsley
- Salt
- Pepper

DIRECTIONS

1. Cook the potato slices in the oil for 10 minutes.
2. Add the zucchini and bell peppers and cook for another 5 minutes.
3. Whisk the eggs in a bowl.
4. Season with salt and pepper and add it to the veggies.
5. Cook on low for 10 minutes.
6. Serve topped with fresh parsley.

SWEET POTATO BREAKFAST CAKE

Serves: *4*
Prep Time: *30*   Minutes

Cook Time: *15*   Minutes

Total Time: *35*   Minutes

INGREDIENTS

- 2 tbs oil
- 2 tbs parsley
- 1 red onion
- 3 egg whites
- 2 sweet potatoes
- ½ cup dried cranberries
- 6 eggs
- Salt
- Pepper

DIRECTIONS

1. Preheat the oven to 425F.
2. Poke holes all around the potatoes using a fork.
3. Add the cranberries, parsley, onion, salt, and pepper.
4. Add 2 whisked egg whites.
5. Make patties from the mixture.
6. Cook in oil for 4 minutes on each side.

7. Place the cooked patties onto a greased baking dish.

8. Push down in the middle of each patty, creating space for the eggs.

9. Crack the eggs on top, into the created space.

10. Bake for 15 minutes.

11. Caramelize the onion in a skillet.

12. Serve topped with the caramelized onions.

MINI EGG OMELETS

Serves: **4**

Prep Time: **10** Minutes

Cook Time: **20** Minutes

Total Time: **30** Minutes

INGREDIENTS

- ¼ cup shredded cheddar
- 4 eggs
- ¼ cup cheese
- 1 ½ tsp olive oil
- 4 cups broccoli florets
- Salt
- Pepper
- 1 cup egg whites

DIRECTIONS

1. Preheat the oven to 350F.
2. Steam the broccoli for 5 minutes.
3. Once cooked, crumble into smaller pieces and add olive oil, salt, and pepper.
4. Grease a muffin tin and pour the mixture into each tin.
5. Beat the egg whites, eggs, cheese, salt and pepper in a bowl.
6. Pour over the broccoli, top with cheese and cook for 20 minutes.

BREAKFAST MEATCAKES

Serves: **14**

Prep Time: **10** Minutes

Cook Time: **40** Minutes

Total Time: **50** Minutes

INGREDIENTS

- 1 lb pork sausage
- 6 ounces blackberries
- 1 tsp cinnamon
- 1 ½ tsp salt
- 1 tsp black pepper
- 1 tsp rosemary
- 1 tsp thyme
- 1 orange zest
- 1 ln chicken breast
- 12 strips bacon
- 1 apple
- 1 tsp garlic powder

DIRECTIONS

1. Preheat the oven to 375F.
2. Dice the apple.
3. Line the cupcake pans with bacon.

4. Mix together, smashing with hands, sausage, spices, chicken, apple, zest, and blackberries.

5. Fill the pan with the mixture.

6. Bake for 35 minutes.

7. Serve topped with zest or blackberries.

CANTALOUPE PANCAKES

Serves: *4*

Prep Time: *10* Minutes

Cook Time: *20* Minutes

Total Time: *30* Minutes

INGREDIENTS

- 1 cup whole wheat flour
- ¼ tsp baking soda
- ¼ tsp baking powder
- 2 eggs
- 1 cup milk
- 1 cup cantaloupe

DIRECTIONS

1. In a bowl combine all ingredients together and mix well
2. In a skillet heat olive oil
3. Pour ¼ of the batter and cook each pancake for 1-2 minutes per side
4. When ready remove from heat and serve

COCONUT PANCAKES

Serves: *4*

Prep Time: *10*   Minutes

Cook Time: *20*   Minutes

Total Time: *30*   Minutes

INGREDIENTS

- 1 cup whole wheat flour
- ¼ tsp baking soda
- ¼ tsp baking powder
- 1 cup coconut flalkes
- 2 eggs
- 1 cup milk

DIRECTIONS

1. In a bowl combine all ingredients together and mix well
2. In a skillet heat olive oil
3. Pour ¼ of the batter and cook each pancake for 1-2 minutes per side
4. When ready remove from heat and serve

CHERRIES PANCAKES

Serves: **4**

Prep Time: **10**   Minutes

Cook Time: **30**   Minutes

Total Time: **40**   Minutes

INGREDIENTS

- 1 cup whole wheat flour
- ¼ tsp baking soda
- ¼ tsp baking powder
- 2 eggs
- 1 cup milk
- 1 cup cherries

DIRECTIONS

1. In a bowl combine all ingredients together and mix well
2. In a skillet heat olive oil
3. Pour ¼ of the batter and cook each pancake for 1-2 minutes per side
4. When ready remove from heat and serve

MANGO MUFFINS

Serves: *8-12*

Prep Time: *10* Minutes

Cook Time: *20* Minutes

Total Time: *30* Minutes

INGREDIENTS

- 2 eggs
- 1 tablespoon olive oil
- 1 cup milk
- 2 cups whole wheat flour
- 1 tsp baking soda
- ¼ tsp baking soda
- 1 tsp ginger
- 1 tsp cinnamon
- 1 cup mango

DIRECTIONS

1. In a bowl combine all wet ingredients
2. In another bowl combine all dry ingredients
3. Combine wet and dry ingredients together
4. Pour mixture into 8-12 prepared muffin cups, fill 2/3 of the cups
5. Bake for 18-20 minutes at 375 F, when ready remove and serve

NECTARINE MUFFINS

Serves: **8-12**
Prep Time: **10**   Minutes

Cook Time: **20**   Minutes

Total Time: **30**   Minutes

INGREDIENTS

- 2 eggs
- 1 tablespoon olive oil
- 1 cup milk
- 2 cups whole wheat flour
- 1 tsp baking soda
- ¼ tsp baking soda
- 1 tsp cinnamon
- 1 cup nectarine

DIRECTIONS

1. In a bowl combine all wet ingredients
2. In another bowl combine all dry ingredients
3. Combine wet and dry ingredients together
4. Pour mixture into 8-12 prepared muffin cups, fill 2/3 of the cups
5. Bake for 18-20 minutes at 375 F
6. When ready remove from the oven and serve

PAPAYA MUFFINS

Serves:	*8-12*
Prep Time:	*10* Minutes
Cook Time:	*20* Minutes
Total Time:	*30* Minutes

INGREDIENTS

- 2 eggs
- 1 tablespoon olive oil
- 1 cup milk
- 2 cups whole wheat flour
- 1 tsp baking soda
- ¼ tsp baking soda
- 1 tsp cinnamon
- 1 cup papaya

DIRECTIONS

1. In a bowl combine all wet ingredients
2. In another bowl combine all dry ingredients
3. Combine wet and dry ingredients together
4. Pour mixture into 8-12 prepared muffin cups, fill 2/3 of the cups
5. Bake for 18-20 minutes at 375 F
6. When ready remove from the oven and serve

PLANTAIN MUFFINS

Serves: **8-12**

Prep Time: **10** Minutes

Cook Time: **20** Minutes

Total Time: **30** Minutes

INGREDIENTS

- 2 eggs
- 1 tablespoon olive oil
- 1 cup milk
- 2 cups whole wheat flour
- 1 tsp baking soda
- ¼ tsp baking soda
- 1 tsp cinnamon
- 1 cup plantain

DIRECTIONS

1. In a bowl combine all wet ingredients
2. In another bowl combine all dry ingredients
3. Combine wet and dry ingredients together
4. Pour mixture into 8-12 prepared muffin cups, fill 2/3 of the cups
5. Bake for 18-20 minutes at 375 F
6. When ready remove from the oven and serve

ONION OMELETTE

Serves: *1*

Prep Time: *5*   Minutes

Cook Time: *10*   Minutes

Total Time: *15*   Minutes

INGREDIENTS

- 2 eggs
- ¼ tsp salt
- ¼ tsp black pepper
- 1 tablespoon olive oil
- ¼ cup cheese
- ¼ tsp basil
- 1 cup red onion

DIRECTIONS

1. In a bowl combine all ingredients together and mix well
2. In a skillet heat olive oil and pour the egg mixture
3. Cook for 1-2 minutes per side
4. When ready remove omelette from the skillet and serve

BEETROOT OMELETTE

Serves: **1**

Prep Time: **5**   Minutes

Cook Time: **10**   Minutes

Total Time: **15**   Minutes

INGREDIENTS

- 2 eggs
- ¼ tsp salt
- ¼ tsp black pepper
- 1 tablespoon olive oil
- ¼ cup cheese
- ¼ tsp basil
- 1 cup mushrooms

DIRECTIONS

1. In a bowl combine all ingredients together and mix well
2. In a skillet heat olive oil and pour the egg mixture
3. Cook for 1-2 minutes per side
4. When ready remove omelette from the skillet and serve

BELL PEPPER OMELETTE

Serves: *1*

Prep Time: *5*   Minutes

Cook Time: *10*   Minutes

Total Time: *15*   Minutes

INGREDIENTS

- 2 eggs
- ¼ tsp salt
- ¼ tsp black pepper
- 1 tablespoon olive oil
- ¼ cup cheese
- ¼ tsp basil
- 1 cup yellow bell pepper

DIRECTIONS

1. In a bowl combine all ingredients together and mix well
2. In a skillet heat olive oil and pour the egg mixture
3. Cook for 1-2 minutes per side
4. When ready remove omelette from the skillet and serve

PEAR TART

Serves: *6-8*
Prep Time: *25*   Minutes

Cook Time: *25*   Minutes

Total Time: *50*   Minutes

INGREDIENTS

- 1 lb. pears
- 2 oz. brown sugar
- ½ lb. flaked almonds
- ¼ lb. porridge oat
- 2 oz. flour
- ¼ lb. almonds
- pastry sheets
- 2 tablespoons syrup

DIRECTIONS

1. Preheat oven to 400 F, unfold pastry sheets and place them on a baking sheet
2. Toss together all ingredients together and mix well

3. Spread mixture in a single layer on the pastry sheets
4. Before baking decorate with your desired fruits
5. Bake at 400 F for 22-25 minutes or until golden brown
6. When ready remove from the oven and serve

CARDAMOM TART

Serves: **6-8**

Prep Time: **25**   Minutes

Cook Time: **25**   Minutes

Total Time: **50**   Minutes

INGREDIENTS

- 4-5 pears
- 2 tablespoons lemon juice
- pastry sheets

CARDAMOM FILLING

- ½ lb. butter
- ½ lb. brown sugar
- ½ lb. almonds
- ¼ lb. flour
- 1 ¼ tsp cardamom
- 2 eggs

DIRECTIONS

1. Preheat oven to 400 F, unfold pastry sheets and place them on a baking sheet
2. Toss together all ingredients together and mix well
3. Spread mixture in a single layer on the pastry sheets
4. Before baking decorate with your desired fruits

5. Bake at 400 F for 22-25 minutes or until golden brown
6. When ready remove from the oven and serve

PEACH PECAN PIE

Serves: *8-12*

Prep Time: *15*   Minutes

Cook Time: *35*   Minutes

Total Time: *50*   Minutes

INGREDIENTS

- 4-5 cups peaches
- 1 tablespoon preserves
- 1 cup sugar
- 4 small egg yolks
- ¼ cup flour
- 1 tsp vanilla extract

DIRECTIONS

1. Line a pie plate or pie form with pastry and cover the edges of the plate depending on your preference
2. In a bowl combine all pie ingredients together and mix well
3. Pour the mixture over the pastry
4. Bake at 400-425 F for 25-30 minutes or until golden brown
5. When ready remove from the oven and let it rest for 15 minutes

BUTTERFINGER PIE

Serves: *8-12*

Prep Time: *15*   Minutes

Cook Time: *35*   Minutes

Total Time: *50*   Minutes

INGREDIENTS

- pastry sheets
- 1 package cream cheese
- 1 tsp vanilla extract
- ¼ cup peanut butter
- 1 cup powdered sugar (to decorate)
- 2 cups Butterfinger candy bars
- 8 oz whipped topping

DIRECTIONS

1. Line a pie plate or pie form with pastry and cover the edges of the plate depending on your preference
2. In a bowl combine all pie ingredients together and mix well
3. Pour the mixture over the pastry
4. Bake at 400-425 F for 25-30 minutes or until golden brown
5. When ready remove from the oven and let it rest for 15 minutes

STRAWBERRY PIE

Serves: *8-12*

Prep Time: *15*   Minutes

Cook Time: *35*   Minutes

Total Time: *50*   Minutes

INGREDIENTS

- pastry sheets
- 1,5 lb. strawberries
- 1 cup powdered sugar
- 2 tablespoons cornstarch
- 1 tablespoon lime juice
- 1 tsp vanilla extract
- 2 eggs
- 2 tablespoons butter

DIRECTIONS

1. Line a pie plate or pie form with pastry and cover the edges of the plate depending on your preference
2. In a bowl combine all pie ingredients together and mix well
3. Pour the mixture over the pastry
4. Bake at 400-425 F for 25-30 minutes or until golden brown
5. When ready remove from the oven and let it rest for 15 minutes

BLUEBERRY PIE

Serves: *8-12*

Prep Time: *15*   Minutes

Cook Time: *35*   Minutes

Total Time: *50*   Minutes

INGREDIENTS

- pastry sheets
- ¼ tsp lavender
- 1 cup brown sugar
- 4-5 cups blueberries
- 1 tablespoon lemon juice
- 1 cup almonds
- 2 tablespoons butter

DIRECTIONS

1. Line a pie plate or pie form with pastry and cover the edges of the plate depending on your preference
2. In a bowl combine all pie ingredients together and mix well
3. Pour the mixture over the pastry
4. Bake at 400-425 F for 25-30 minutes or until golden brown
5. When ready remove from the oven and let it rest for 15 minutes

GINGER-OAT SMOOTHIE

Serves: *1*

Prep Time: *5*   Minutes

Cook Time: *5*   Minutes

Total Time: *10*   Minutes

INGREDIENTS

- ½ cup oats
- ¼ cup blueberries
- ¼ cup vanilla yogurt
- 1 cup ice
- ¼ tsp ginger

DIRECTIONS

1. In a blender place all ingredients and blend until smooth
2. Pour smoothie in a glass and serve

PUMPKIN SMOOTHIE

Serves: *1*
Prep Time: 5   Minutes

Cook Time: 5   Minutes

Total Time: *10*   Minutes

INGREDIENTS

- 1 cup ice
- 1 cup almond milk
- ½ cup pumpkin puree
- 1 tsp honey

DIRECTIONS

1. In a blender place all ingredients and blend until smooth
2. Pour smoothie in a glass and serve

GREEN SMOOTHIE

Serves: **1**

Prep Time: **5**   Minutes

Cook Time: **5**   Minutes

Total Time: **10**   Minutes

INGREDIENTS

- 1 cup kale
- 1 celery
- 1 banana
- 1 cup apple juice
- 1 cup ice

DIRECTIONS

1. In a blender place all ingredients and blend until smooth
2. Pour smoothie in a glass and serve

MANGO SMOOTHIE

Serves: *1*

Prep Time: *5*   Minutes

Cook Time: *5*   Minutes

Total Time: *10* Minutes

INGREDIENTS

- 1 cup mango
- ½ cup coconut milk
- 1 cup ice
- ½ cup vanilla yogurt
- 1 tsp honey

DIRECTIONS

1. In a blender place all ingredients and blend until smooth
2. Pour smoothie in a glass and serve

PINEAPPLE SMOOTHIE

Serves: **1**
Prep Time: **5**   Minutes

Cook Time: **5**   Minutes

Total Time: **10** Minutes

INGREDIENTS

- 1 cup pineapple
- 1 cup ice
- 1 orange juice
- ½ cup carrot
- 1 banana

DIRECTIONS

1. In a blender place all ingredients and blend until smooth
2. Pour smoothie in a glass and serve

CASHEW SMOOTHIE

Serves: *1*
Prep Time: 5   Minutes

Cook Time: 5   Minutes

Total Time: *10*   Minutes

INGREDIENTS

- 1 cup cashews
- 1 cup ice
- 1 banana
- 1 tablespoon honey

DIRECTIONS

1. In a blender place all ingredients and blend until smooth
2. Pour smoothie in a glass and serve

NUT SMOOTHIE

Serves: *1*

Prep Time: 5   Minutes

Cook Time: 5   Minutes

Total Time: *10*   Minutes

INGREDIENTS

- 1 cup coconut milk
- 1 cup raspberries
- 1 banana
- 1 tablespoon peanut butter
- 1 tsp agave nectar

DIRECTIONS

1. In a blender place all ingredients and blend until smooth
2. Pour smoothie in a glass and serve

STRAWBERRY SMOOTHIE

Serves: *1*

Prep Time: 5   Minutes

Cook Time: 5   Minutes

Total Time: *10*   Minutes

INGREDIENTS

- 1 cup strawberries
- 1 cup Greek Yoghurt
- ½ cup orange juice
- 1 tsp honey
- 1 tablespoon flaxseed meal

DIRECTIONS

1. In a blender place all ingredients and blend until smooth
2. Pour smoothie in a glass and serve

SPINACH & GRAPE SMOOTHIE

Serves: *1*

Prep Time: *5*   Minutes

Cook Time: *5*   Minutes

Total Time: *10*   Minutes

INGREDIENTS

- 1 cup grapes
- 1 cup baby spinach
- 1 cup ice
- 1 cup almond milk

DIRECTIONS

1. In a blender place all ingredients and blend until smooth
2. Pour smoothie in a glass and serve

ICE-CREAM RECIPES

SAFFRON ICE-CREAM

Serves: **6-8**

Prep Time: **15** Minutes
Cook Time: **15** Minutes
Total Time: **30** Minutes

INGREDIENTS

- 4 egg yolks
- 1 cup heavy cream
- 1 cup milk
- ½ cup brown sugar
- 1 tsp saffron
- 1 tsp vanilla extract

DIRECTIONS

1. In a saucepan whisk together all ingredients
2. Mix until bubbly
3. Strain into a bowl and cool
4. Whisk in favorite fruits and mix well
5. Cover and refrigerate for 2-3 hours

6. Pour mixture in the ice-cream maker and follow manufacturer instructions
7. Serve when ready

PISTACHIOS ICE-CREAM

Serves: **6-8**

Prep Time: **15**   Minutes

Cook Time: **15**   Minutes

Total Time: **30**   Minutes

INGREDIENTS

- 4 egg yolks
- 1 cup heavy cream
- 1 cup milk
- 1 cup sugar
- 1 vanilla bean
- 1 tsp almond extract
- 1 cup cherries
- ½ cup pistachios

DIRECTIONS

1. In a saucepan whisk together all ingredients
2. Mix until bubbly
3. Strain into a bowl and cool
4. Whisk in favorite fruits and mix well
5. Cover and refrigerate for 2-3 hours
6. Pour mixture in the ice-cream maker and follow manufacturer instructions

VANILLA ICE-CREAM

Serves: *6-8*

Prep Time: *15*   Minutes
Cook Time: *15*   Minutes
Total Time: *30*   Minutes

INGREDIENTS

- 1 cup milk
- 1 tablespoon cornstarch
- 1 oz. cream cheese
- 1 cup heavy cream
- 1 cup brown sugar
- 1 tablespoon corn syrup
- 1 vanilla bean

DIRECTIONS

1. In a saucepan whisk together all ingredients
2. Mix until bubbly
3. Strain into a bowl and cool
4. Whisk in favorite fruits and mix well
5. Cover and refrigerate for 2-3 hours
6. Pour mixture in the ice-cream maker and follow manufacturer instructions
7. Serve when ready

THIRD COOKBOOK

SPICY SHRIMP STIR FRY

Serves: *1*

Prep Time: *10* Minutes

Cook Time: *10* Minutes

Total Time: *20* Minutes

INGREDIENTS

- 1 orange
- Cayenne powder
- 3 oz shrimp
- Ginger powder
- 4 tbs vegetable stock
- Curry powder
- 25 cups red onion
- 1 cup cabbage
- Garlic powder

DIRECTIONS

1. Coat the shrimp in the seasonings.
2. Pour the broth into a pan, then add cabbage, onion, and shrimp.
3. Cook until the shrimp turns pink.
4. Serve topped with orange juice and orange slices.

ARTICHOKE AND SPINACH PIZZA

Serves:	*6-8*	
Prep Time:	*10*	Minutes
Cook Time:	*15*	Minutes
Total Time:	*25*	Minutes

INGREDIENTS

- 1 pizza crust
- 1 garlic clove
- ½ lb. spinach
- ½ lb. soft cheese
- 2 oz. artichoke hearts
- 1 cup mozzarella cheese
- 1 tablespoon olive oil

DIRECTIONS

1. Spread tomato sauce on the pizza crust
2. Place all the toppings on the pizza crust
3. Bake the pizza at 425 F for 12-15 minutes
4. When ready remove pizza from the oven and serve

MINT PIZZA

Serves: *6-8*
Prep Time: *10*   Minutes

Cook Time: *15*   Minutes

Total Time: *25*   Minutes

INGREDIENTS

- 1 pizza crust
- 1 olive oil
- 1 garlic clove
- 1 cup mozzarella cheese
- 2 oz. mint
- 2 courgettes

DIRECTIONS

1. Spread tomato sauce on the pizza crust
2. Place all the toppings on the pizza crust
3. Bake the pizza at 425 F for 12-15 minutes
4. When ready remove pizza from the oven and serve

SAUSAGE PIZZA

Serves: **6-8**

Prep Time: **10** Minutes

Cook Time: **15** Minutes

Total Time: **25** Minutes

INGREDIENTS

- 2 pork sausages
- 1 tablespoon olive oil
- 2 garlic cloves
- 1 tsp fennel seeds
- ½ lb. ricotta
- 1 cup mozzarella cheese
- 1 oz. parmesan cheese
- 1 pizza crust

DIRECTIONS

1. Spread tomato sauce on the pizza crust
2. Place all the toppings on the pizza crust
3. Bake the pizza at 425 F for 12-15 minutes
4. When ready remove pizza from the oven and serve

BEEF & BROCCOLI STIR FRY

Serves: **4**

Prep Time: **10**   Minutes

Cook Time: **30**   Minutes

Total Time: **40**   Minutes

INGREDIENTS

- 2 cloves garlic
- ½ lb Beef Sirloin steaks
- Chicken broth
- 2 tbs liquid Aminos
- 1 tsp onion powder
- 1 tbs parsley
- 2 cups broccoli florets

DIRECTIONS

1. Sauté the beef in a few tbs of chicken broth until brown.
2. Add onion powder, garlic, broccoli, liquid aminos and parsley.
3. Saute until well done.
4. Serve immediately.

GINGER CHICKEN SOUP

Serves: *1*
Prep Time: *5*   Minutes

Cook Time: *15*   Minutes

Total Time: *20*   Minutes

INGREDIENTS

- 2 cloves garlic
- Salt
- Pepper
- 3 stalks celery
- 3 oz chicken tenders
- 4 cups chicken broth
- 4 slices ginger

DIRECTIONS

1. Bring the broth to a boil.
2. Add the garlic, ginger, and celery.
3. Simmer for 5 minutes.
4. Add in the chicken and boil for 10 more minutes.
5. Season with salt and pepper.
6. Serve immediately.

CILANTRO SKEWERS

Serves: *1*

Prep Time: *20*   Minutes

Cook Time: *120*   Minutes

Total Time: *140*   Minutes

INGREDIENTS

- Cherry tomatoes
- Red pepper flakes
- Salt
- Pepper
- 2 tbs lemon juice
- Cilantro
- 100g shrimp

DIRECTIONS

1. Mix the cilantro, red pepper flakes, salt, pepper and shrimp together.
2. Marinade for at least 2 hours.
3. Place on skewers alternating with tomatoes.
4. Cook on a barbeque.
5. Season with salt and pepper.
6. Serve immediately.

CURRY SHRIMP

Serves: *14*
Prep Time: *10*   Minutes

Cook Time: *10*   Minutes

Total Time: *20*   Minutes

INGREDIENTS

- 1/8 cup water
- 100g shrimp
- 1 onion
- Pepper
- 1/ tsp curry powder
- ¼ tsp cumin
- Salt
- 4 garlic cloves

DIRECTIONS

1. Cook the garlic and onion until translucent.
2. Add in the shrimp, seasonings and water.
3. Cook until done.
4. Serve immediately.

Serves: *1*
Prep Time: *10* Minutes

Cook Time: *15* Minutes

Total Time: *25* Minutes

INGREDIENTS

- 100g orange roughy fillet
- 2 tbs lemon juice
- 1 tsp thyme
- 1 tsp rosemary
- ¼ tsp onion powder
- Salt
- Pepper

DIRECTIONS

1. Place the ingredients in a baking dish and cover with tin foil.
2. Bake at 350F for 15 minutes.
3. Serve hot.

LEMON TILAPIA

Serves: **1**

Prep Time: **10** Minutes

Cook Time: **20** Minutes

Total Time: **30** Minutes

INGREDIENTS

- ¼ cup lemon juice
- 1 lemon zest
- 100g tilapia
- 1 tbs onion
- 1 tsp dill
- Salt
- Pepper

DIRECTIONS

1. Place the ingredients in a tin foil, then wrap them up.
2. Cook on a grill until done
3. Serve when ready

MEDITERRANEAN SEA BASS

Serves: **1**

Prep Time: **10**   Minutes

Cook Time: **10**   Minutes

Total Time: **20**   Minutes

INGREDIENTS

- 100g sea Bass
- 2 cloves garlic
- 1 lemon juice
- 1 lemon zest
- 1 tbs onion
- ½ tsp parsley
- Salt
- Pepper

DIRECTIONS

1. Place the ingredients in a tin foil bag.
2. Cook on the barbeque for 10 minutes.
3. Serve topped with fresh parsley.

WASABI WHITEFISH

Serves: **1**

Prep Time: **10** Minutes

Cook Time: **5** Minutes

Total Time: **15** Minutes

INGREDIENTS

- ½ tsp ginger
- 100g whitefish
- 1 tbs mustard
- 1 tsp wasabi powder

DIRECTIONS

1. Mix the mustard with the wasabi powder.
2. Add the ginger.
3. Coat the fish with the mixture.
4. Allow to sit for at least half an hour.
5. Grill for 5 minutes.
6. Serve hot.

CAJUN CHICKEN

Serves: *1*

Prep Time: **5**   Minutes

Cook Time: **25** Minutes

Total Time: *30* Minutes

INGREDIENTS

- ½ tbs milk
- ½ tsp Cajun seasoning
- 100g chicken

DIRECTIONS

1. Preheat the oven to 350F.
2. Coat the chicken with milk.
3. Sprinkle with Cajun seasoning.
4. Bake for 25 minutes.
5. Serve immediately.

Serves: *1*
Prep Time: *5*   Minutes

Cook Time: *0*   Minutes

Total Time: *5*   Minutes

INGREDIENTS

- ½ tomato
- 1 toast
- 100g chicken
- Basil
- Salt
- Pepper

DIRECTIONS

1. Cook the chicken, allow to chill, then shred.
2. Arrange the ingredients on top of the toast.
3. Serve immediately.

MARINARA CHICKEN

Serves: *1*
Prep Time: *10*   Minutes

Cook Time: *25*   Minutes

Total Time: *35*   Minutes

INGREDIENTS

- ½ tsp oregano
- Parsley
- 100g chicken
- 1 toast
- ½ tsp basil
- 3 garlic cloves
- 2 tsp onion
- Salt
- Pepper

DIRECTIONS

1. Crush the toast and combine with oregano, basil, salt, and pepper.
2. Coat the chicken with the mixture and place in a casserole dish.
3. Cook covered for 25 minutes at 375F.
4. Serve topped with marinara sauce and parsley.

EDAMAME FRITATTA

Serves: **2**

Prep Time: **10**   Minutes

Cook Time: **20**   Minutes

Total Time: **30**   Minutes

INGREDIENTS

- 1 cup edamame
- 1 tablespoon olive oil
- ½ red onion
- 2 eggs
- ¼ tsp salt
- 2 oz. cheddar cheese
- 1 garlic clove
- ¼ tsp dill

DIRECTIONS

1. In a bowl whisk eggs with salt and cheese
2. In a frying pan heat olive oil and pour egg mixture
3. Add remaining ingredients and mix well
4. Serve when ready

LEEKS FRITATTA

Serves: **2**
Prep Time: **10** Minutes

Cook Time: **20** Minutes

Total Time: **30** Minutes

INGREDIENTS

- ½ lb. leek
- 1 tablespoon olive oil
- ½ red onion
- ¼ tsp salt
- 2 eggs
- 2 oz. cheddar cheese
- 1 garlic clove
- ¼ tsp dill

DIRECTIONS

1. In a bowl whisk eggs with salt and cheese
2. In a frying pan heat olive oil and pour egg mixture
3. Add remaining ingredients and mix well
4. Serve when ready

MUSHROOM FRITATTA

Serves: **2**

Prep Time: **10** Minutes

Cook Time: **20** Minutes

Total Time: **30** Minutes

INGREDIENTS

- ½ lb. mushrooms
- 1 tablespoon olive oil
- ½ red onion
- ¼ tsp salt
- 2 eggs
- 2 oz. cheddar cheese
- 1 garlic clove
- ¼ tsp dill

DIRECTIONS

1. In a bowl whisk eggs with salt and cheese
2. In a frying pan heat olive oil and pour egg mixture
3. Add remaining ingredients and mix well
4. Serve when ready

PEAS FRITATTA

Serves: *2*
Prep Time: *10* Minutes

Cook Time: *20* Minutes

Total Time: *30* Minutes

INGREDIENTS

- 1 cup peas
- 1 tablespoon olive oil
- ½ red onion
- ¼ tsp salt
- 2 eggs
- 2 oz. cheddar cheese
- 1 garlic clove
- ¼ tsp dill

DIRECTIONS

1. In a bowl whisk eggs with salt and cheese
2. In a frying pan heat olive oil and pour egg mixture
3. Add remaining ingredients and mix well
4. Serve when ready.

BELL PEPPER FRITATTA

Serves: **2**

Prep Time: **10**   Minutes

Cook Time: **20**   Minutes

Total Time: **30**   Minutes

INGREDIENTS

- 1 cup red bell pepper
- 1 tablespoon olive oil
- ½ red onion
- ¼ tsp salt
- 2 eggs
- 2 oz. parmesan cheese
- 1 garlic clove
- ¼ tsp dill

DIRECTIONS

1. In a bowl whisk eggs with salt and cheese
2. In a frying pan heat olive oil and pour egg mixture
3. Add remaining ingredients and mix well
4. Serve when ready.

POTATO FRITATTA

Serves: *2*
Prep Time: *10*   Minutes

Cook Time: *20*   Minutes

Total Time: *30*   Minutes

INGREDIENTS

- 1 cup sweet potato
- 1 tablespoon olive oil
- ½ red onion
- ¼ tsp salt
- 2 eggs
- 2 oz. cheddar cheese
- 1 garlic clove
- ¼ tsp dill

DIRECTIONS

1. In a bowl whisk eggs with salt and cheese
2. In a frying pan heat olive oil and pour egg mixture
3. Add remaining ingredients and mix well
4. Serve when ready

SKILLET PIZZA

Serves: *1*

Prep Time: *10* Minutes

Cook Time: *20* Minutes

Total Time: *30* Minutes

INGREDIENTS

- ¼ red onion
- ½ cup red bell pepper
- ¼ tsp salt
- 2 eggs
- 1 cup tomato sauce
- 1 cup mozzarella cheese
- 1 pizza crust

DIRECTIONS

1. On a pizza crust spread tomato sauce
2. Add toppings on pizza
3. Place pizza in the skillet and cover with a lid
4. Cook on low heat for 18-20 minutes or until pizza is ready

GLAZED PORK CHOPS

Serves: **4**

Prep Time: **10** Minutes

Cook Time: **15** Minutes

Total Time: **25** Minutes

INGREDIENTS

- 1 cup all-purpose flour
- 4 pork loin chops
- ½ cup maple syrup
- 1 tablespoon cornstarch
- 1 cup brown sugar
- pinch of salt
- 2 tablespoons water

DIRECTIONS

1. In a bowl combine salt and flour together
2. Place the pork chops in the bowl and turn to coat
3. Place pork chops in a skillet and cook until golden brown
4. Add maple syrup, sugar, water cornstarch, and bring to a boil
5. Cook until the sugar is dissolved and meat is cooked
6. When ready remove from the skillet and serve

PANINI CHICKEN

Serves: *1*
Prep Time: *10*   Minutes

Cook Time: *15*   Minutes

Total Time: *25*   Minutes

INGREDIENTS

- 1 lb. chicken breast
- 1 tsp gingerroot
- ½ cup chicken broth
- ¼ tsp salt
- ¼ tsp turmeric
- 4 green onion

DIRECTIONS

1. In a slow cooker place your chicken and add broth, garlic clove, green onions and gingerroot
2. When ready remove chicken mixture and place the chicken on a flatbread
3. Cook sandwich in a panini maker
4. When ready remove and serve

PENNE PASTA

Serves: *2*
Prep Time: *10*   Minutes

Cook Time: *20*   Minutes

Total Time: *30*   Minutes

INGREDIENTS

- 1 package penne pasta
- 1 onion
- 1 tablespoon thyme
- 1 tablespoon basil
- ¼ cup white wine
- 1 tablespoon tomato paste
- 1 tablespoon all-purpose flour
- 1 cup parmesan cheese

DIRECTIONS

1. In a stockpot cook pasta al dente
2. In a skillet sauté onion until soft, add salt, herbs, tomato paste, flour and cook for 2-3 minutes
3. Add pasta to the tomato mixture and bring to a boil
4. When ready serve with parmesan cheese on top

TURKEY SANDWICH

Serves: *1*
Prep Time: *5*   Minutes

Cook Time: *5*   Minutes

Total Time: *10*   Minutes

INGREDIENTS

- 2 oz. cream cheese
- 2 tablespoons salad dressing
- 1 tsp garlic powder
- 1 loaf bread
- Lettuce
- 1 lb. cooked turkey
- ½ lb. swiss cheese
- 1 tomato

DIRECTIONS

1. In a bowl combine cream cheese, garlic powder and salad dressing
2. Spread mixture on the bread
3. Add lettuce, tomatoes, cheese and turkey
4. Serve when ready

ROASTED SQUASH

Serves: **3-4**

Prep Time: **10** Minutes

Cook Time: **20** Minutes

Total Time: **30** Minutes

INGREDIENTS

- 2 delicata squashes
- 2 tablespoons olive oil
- 1 tsp curry powder
- 1 tsp salt

DIRECTIONS

1. Preheat the oven to 400 F
2. Cut everything in half lengthwise
3. Toss everything with olive oil and place onto a prepared baking sheet
4. Roast for 18-20 minutes at 400 F or until golden brown
5. When ready remove from the oven and serve

BRUSSELS SPROUT CHIPS

Serves: **2**
Prep Time: **10** Minutes

Cook Time: **20** Minutes

Total Time: **30** Minutes

INGREDIENTS

- 1 lb. brussels sprouts
- 1 tablespoon olive oil
- 1 tablespoon parmesan cheese
- 1 tsp garlic powder
- 1 tsp seasoning

DIRECTIONS

1. Preheat the oven to 425 F
2. In a bowl toss everything with olive oil and seasoning
3. Spread everything onto a prepared baking sheet
4. Bake for 8-10 minutes or until crisp
5. When ready remove from the oven and serve

BEET CHIPS

Serves: **2**

Prep Time: **10**   Minutes

Cook Time: **20**   Minutes

Total Time: **30**   Minutes

INGREDIENTS

- 1 lb. beet
- 1 tablespoon olive oil
- 1 tablespoon parmesan cheese
- 1 tsp garlic powder
- 1 tsp seasoning

DIRECTIONS

1. Preheat the oven to 425 F
2. In a bowl toss everything with olive oil and seasoning
3. Spread everything onto a prepared baking sheet
4. Bake for 8-10 minutes or until crisp
5. When ready remove from the oven and serve

SPINACH CHIPS

Serves: *2*

Prep Time: *10*   Minutes

Cook Time: *20*   Minutes

Total Time: *30*   Minutes

INGREDIENTS

- 1 lb. spinach
- 1 tablespoon olive oil
- 1 tablespoon parmesan cheese
- 1 tsp garlic powder
- 1 tsp seasoning

DIRECTIONS

1. Preheat the oven to 425 F
2. In a bowl toss everything with olive oil and seasoning
3. Spread everything onto a prepared baking sheet
4. Bake for 8-10 minutes or until crisp
5. When ready remove from the oven and serve

KALE CHIPS

Serves: **2**

Prep Time: **10** Minutes

Cook Time: **20** Minutes

Total Time: **30** Minutes

INGREDIENTS

- 1 lb. kale
- 1 tablespoon olive oil
- 1 tablespoon parmesan cheese
- 1 tsp garlic powder
- 1 tsp seasoning

DIRECTIONS

1. Preheat the oven to 425 F
2. In a bowl toss everything with olive oil and seasoning
3. Spread everything onto a prepared baking sheet
4. Bake for 8-10 minutes or until crisp
5. When ready remove from the oven and serve

EGGPLANT CHIPS

Serves: *2*
Prep Time: *10*   Minutes

Cook Time: *20*   Minutes

Total Time: *30*   Minutes

INGREDIENTS

- 1 lb. eggplant
- 1 tablespoon olive oil
- 1 tablespoon parmesan cheese
- 1 tsp garlic powder
- 1 tsp seasoning

DIRECTIONS

1. Preheat the oven to 425 F
2. In a bowl toss everything with olive oil and seasoning
3. Spread everything onto a prepared baking sheet
4. Bake for 8-10 minutes or until crisp
5. When ready remove from the oven and serve

TOMATO CHIPS

Serves: *2*
Prep Time: *10*   Minutes

Cook Time: *20*   Minutes

Total Time: *30*   Minutes

INGREDIENTS

- 1 lb. tomato
- 1 tablespoon olive oil
- 1 tablespoon parmesan cheese
- 1 tsp garlic powder
- 1 tsp seasoning

DIRECTIONS

1. Preheat the oven to 425 F
2. In a bowl toss everything with olive oil and seasoning
3. Spread everything onto a prepared baking sheet
4. Bake for 8-10 minutes or until crisp
5. When ready remove from the oven and serve

PASTA

SIMPLE SPAGHETTI

Serves: 2

Prep Time: 5   Minutes

Cook Time: 15   Minutes

Total Time: 20   Minutes

INGREDIENTS

- 10 oz. spaghetti
- 2 eggs
- ½ cup parmesan cheese
- 1 tsp black pepper
- Olive oil
- 1 tsp parsley
- 2 cloves garlic

DIRECTIONS

1. In a pot boil spaghetti (or any other type of pasta), drain and set aside
2. In a bowl whish eggs with parmesan cheese
3. In a skillet heat olive oil, add garlic and cook for 1-2 minutes
4. Pour egg mixture and mix well
5. Add pasta and stir well

6. When ready garnish with parsley and serve

SALAD

COUSCOUS SALAD

Serves: **5**

Prep Time: **10**   Minutes

Cook Time: **50**   Minutes

Total Time: **60**   Minutes

INGREDIENTS
Salad
- Spinach leaves
- Seasonings
- ½ pumpkin
- 1 cup cous cous
- 2 chicken breasts

Dressing
- 2 tbs vinegar
- 3 tbs olive oil
- 2 tbs mustard
- 4 tbs mayonnaise
- 2 tbs lemon juice
- Pepper
- Salt

DIRECTIONS

1. Peel and cut the pumpkin
2. Toss in oil and season
3. Roast in oven for at least 30 minutes
4. Grill the chicken
5. Cook the cous cous
6. Mix the dressing ingredients together
7. Mix everyting together in a salad bowl
8. Serve

POTATO SALAD

Serves: 2

Prep Time: 5   Minutes

Cook Time: 10   Minutes

Total Time: 15   Minutes

INGREDIENTS

- 5 potatoes
- 1 tsp cumin seeds
- 1/3 cup oil
- 2 tsp mustard
- 1 red onion
- 2 cloves garlic
- 1/3 cup lemon juice
- 1 tsp sea salt

DIRECTIONS

1. Steam the potatoes until tender
2. Mix mustard, turmeric powder, lemon juice, cumin seeds, and salt
3. Place the potatoes in a bowl and pour the lemon mixture over
4. Add the chopped onion and minced garlic over
5. Stir to coat and refrigerate covered
6. Add oil and stir before serving

CARROT SALAD

Serves: **2**
Prep Time: **5**   Minutes

Cook Time: **5**   Minutes

Total Time: **10**   Minutes

INGREDIENTS

- 1 ½ tbs lemon juice
- 1/3 tsp salt
- ¼ tsp black pepper
- 2 tbs olive oil
- 1/3 lb carrots
- 1 tsp mustard

DIRECTIONS

1. Mix mustard, lemon juice and oil together
2. Peel and shred the carrots in a bowl
3. Stir in the dressing and season with salt and pepper
4. Mix well and allow to chill for at least 30 minutes
5. Serve

MOROCCAN SALAD

Serves: **2**

Prep Time: **5** Minutes

Cook Time: **5** Minutes

Total Time: **10** Minutes

INGREDIENTS

- 2 tbs lemon juice
- 1 tsp cumin
- 1 tsp paprika
- 3 tbs olive oil
- 2 cloves garlic
- 5 carrots
- Salt
- Pepper

DIRECTIONS

1. Peel and slice the carrots
2. Add the carrots in boiled water and simmer for at least 5 minutes
3. Drain and rinse the carrots under cold water
4. Add in a bowl
5. Mix the lemon juice, garlic, cumin, paprika, and olive oil together

6. Pour the mixture over the carrots and toss then season with salt and pepper
7. Serve immediately

AVOCADO CHICKEN SALAD

Serves: **2**

Prep Time: **5**   Minutes

Cook Time: **5**   Minutes

Total Time: **10** Minutes

INGREDIENTS

- 3 tsp lime juice
- 3 tbs cilantro
- 1 chicken breast
- 1 avocado
- 1/3 cup onion
- 1 apple
- 1 cup celery
- Salt
- Pepper
- Olive oil

DIRECTIONS

1. Dice the chicken breast
2. Season with salt and pepper and cook into a greased skillet until golden
3. Dice the vegetables and place over the chicken in a bowl
4. Mash the avocado and sprinkle in the cilantro

5. Season with salt and pepper and add lime juice
6. Serve drizzled with olive oil

CUCUMBER SALAD

Serves: *8*
Prep Time: 5   Minutes

Cook Time: 5   Minutes

Total Time: *10*   Minutes

INGREDIENTS

- 2 cucumbers
- ½ cup vinegar
- 2 tsp sugar
- 1/3 cup water
- 2 tbs sour cream
- ½ tbs salt
- 1 ½ tsp paprika
- ½ onion

DIRECTIONS

1. Peel and slice the cucumbers
2. Place the cucumbers on a baking sheet and sprinkle with salt
3. Allow to chill for about 30 minutes then squeeze out the excess water
4. Place the onion slices in a bowl and add the drained cucumbers over
5. Add water, sugar, vinegar and paprika

6. Allow to marinate for at least 2 hours
7. Serve

MANGO SALAD

Serves: **4**
Prep Time: **10**   Minutes

Cook Time: **5**   Minutes

Total Time: **15**   Minutes

INGREDIENTS
Salad
- Salad leaves
- 2 chicken breasts
- 2 mangoes
- 2 avocados
- 2 tbs pine nuts

Dressing
- 3 tbs oil
- Salt
- Pepper
- 2 tbs lemon juice
- 3 tbs orange juice
- 1 tsp mustard

DIRECTIONS

1. Divide the salat onto 4 plates
2. Slice the peeled mango and place over the salad
3. Peel and slice the avocado then place it on top

4. Grill the chicken, dice it and place it over
5. Mix the dressing ingredients together and pour over
6. Serve immediately

RICE SALAD

Serves: **4**

Prep Time: **10**   Minutes

Cook Time: **5**   Minutes

Total Time: **15**   Minutes

INGREDIENTS

Salad
- 3 tbs basil leaves
- 100g Kalamata olives
- 3 tbs pine nuts
- 2 green shallots
- ½ sun dried tomato
- 1 cup rice

Dressing
- 3 tbs oil
- Pepper
- 2 tbs mustard
- 3 tbs lemon juice
- Salt
- 1 clove garlic

DIRECTIONS

1. Cook the rice
2. Mix the dressing ingredients together

3. Mix the salad ingredients with the rice in a bowl
4. Add the dressing and serve

FOURTH COOKBOOK

BREAKFAST

PRUNES PANCAKES

Serves: **4**

Prep Time: **10** Minutes

Cook Time: **30** Minutes

Total Time: **40** Minutes

INGREDIENTS

- 1 cup whole wheat flour
- ¼ tsp baking soda
- ¼ tsp baking powder
- 2 eggs
- 1 cup milk
- ½ cup prunes

DIRECTIONS

1. In a bowl combine all ingredients together and mix well
2. In a skillet heat olive oil
3. Pour ¼ of the batter and cook each pancake for 1-2 minutes per side
4. When ready remove from heat and serve

PRUNES MUFFINS

Serves: *8-12*

Prep Time: *10*   Minutes

Cook Time: *20*   Minutes

Total Time: *30*   Minutes

INGREDIENTS

- 2 eggs
- 1 tablespoon olive oil
- 1 cup milk
- 2 cups whole wheat flour
- 1 tsp baking soda
- ¼ tsp baking soda
- 1 cup prunes
- 1 tsp cinnamon
- ¼ cup molasses

DIRECTIONS

1. In a bowl combine all wet ingredients
2. In another bowl combine all dry ingredients
3. Combine wet and dry ingredients together
4. Pour mixture into 8-12 prepared muffin cups, fill 2/3 of the cups
5. Bake for 18-20 minutes at 375 F

PLANTAIN MUFFINS

Serves: *8-12*

Prep Time: *10*   Minutes

Cook Time: *20*   Minutes

Total Time: *30*   Minutes

INGREDIENTS

- 2 eggs
- 1 tablespoon olive oil
- 1 cup milk
- 2 cups whole wheat flour
- 1 tsp baking soda
- ¼ tsp baking soda
- 1 tsp cinnamon
- 1 cup plantain

DIRECTIONS

1. In a bowl combine all wet ingredients
2. In another bowl combine all dry ingredients
3. Combine wet and dry ingredients together
4. Pour mixture into 8-12 prepared muffin cups, fill 2/3 of the cups
5. Bake for 18-20 minutes at 375 F
6. When ready remove from the oven and serve

BLUEBERRY MUFFINS

Serves: *8-12*

Prep Time: *10*   Minutes

Cook Time: *20*   Minutes

Total Time: *30*   Minutes

INGREDIENTS

- 2 eggs
- 1 tablespoon olive oil
- 1 cup milk
- 2 cups whole wheat flour
- 1 tsp baking soda
- ¼ tsp baking soda
- 1 tsp cinnamon
- 1 cup blueberries

DIRECTIONS

1. In a bowl combine all wet ingredients
2. In another bowl combine all dry ingredients
3. Combine wet and dry ingredients together
4. Fold in blueberries and mix well
5. Pour mixture into 8-12 prepared muffin cups, fill 2/3 of the cups
6. Bake for 18-20 minutes at 375 F

PUMPKIN MUFFINS

Serves: *8-12*
Prep Time: *10* Minutes
Cook Time: *20* Minutes
Total Time: *30* Minutes

INGREDIENTS

- 2 eggs
- 1 tablespoon olive oil
- 1 cup milk
- 2 cups whole wheat flour
- 1 tsp baking soda
- ¼ tsp baking soda
- 1 tsp cinnamon
- 1 cup pumpkin puree

DIRECTIONS

1. In a bowl combine all wet ingredients
2. In another bowl combine all dry ingredients
3. Combine wet and dry ingredients together
4. Pour mixture into 8-12 prepared muffin cups, fill 2/3 of the cups
5. Bake for 18-20 minutes at 375 F
6. When ready remove from the oven and serve

CHOCOLATE MUFFINS

Serves: *8-12*
Prep Time: *10*   Minutes

Cook Time: *20*   Minutes

Total Time: *30*   Minutes

INGREDIENTS

- 2 eggs
- 1 tablespoon olive oil
- 1 cup milk
- 2 cups whole wheat flour
- 1 tsp baking soda
- ¼ tsp baking soda
- 1 tsp cinnamon
- 1 cup chocolate chips

DIRECTIONS

1. In a bowl combine all wet ingredients
2. In another bowl combine all dry ingredients
3. Combine wet and dry ingredients together
4. Fold in chocolate chips and mix well
5. Pour mixture into 8-12 prepared muffin cups, fill 2/3 of the cups
6. Bake for 18-20 minutes at 375 F

GOOSEBERRY MUFFINS

Serves: *8-12*

Prep Time: *10*   Minutes

Cook Time: *20*   Minutes

Total Time: *30*   Minutes

INGREDIENTS

- 2 eggs
- 1 tablespoon olive oil
- 1 cup milk
- 2 cups whole wheat flour
- 1 tsp baking soda
- ¼ tsp baking soda
- 1 tsp gooseberries

DIRECTIONS

1. In a bowl combine all wet ingredients
2. In another bowl combine all dry ingredients
3. Combine wet and dry ingredients together
4. Pour mixture into 8-12 prepared muffin cups, fill 2/3 of the cups
5. Bake for 18-20 minutes at 375 F
6. When ready remove from the oven and serve

GOAT CHEESE OMELETTE

Serves: *1*
Prep Time: *5*   Minutes

Cook Time: *10* Minutes

Total Time: *15* Minutes

INGREDIENTS

- 2 eggs
- ¼ tsp salt
- ¼ tsp black pepper
- 1 tablespoon olive oil
- ¼ cup goat cheese
- ¼ tsp basil

DIRECTIONS

1. In a bowl combine all ingredients together and mix well
2. In a skillet heat olive oil and pour the egg mixture
3. Cook for 1-2 minutes per side
4. When ready remove omelette from the skillet and serve

ZUCCHINI OMELETTE

Serves: *1*

Prep Time: *5*   Minutes

Cook Time: *10*   Minutes

Total Time: *15*   Minutes

INGREDIENTS

- 2 eggs
- ¼ tsp salt
- ¼ tsp black pepper
- 1 tablespoon olive oil
- ¼ cup cheese
- ¼ tsp basil
- 1 cup zucchini

DIRECTIONS

1. In a bowl combine all ingredients together and mix well
2. In a skillet heat olive oil and pour the egg mixture
3. Cook for 1-2 minutes per side
4. When ready remove omelette from the skillet and serve

ENCHILADA OMELETTE

Serves: *1*
Prep Time: *5*   Minutes

Cook Time: *10*   Minutes

Total Time: *15*   Minutes

INGREDIENTS

- 2 eggs
- ¼ tsp salt
- ¼ tsp black pepper
- 1 tablespoon olive oil
- ¼ cup cheese
- ¼ tsp basil
- 1 cup enchilada

DIRECTIONS

1. In a bowl combine all ingredients together and mix well
2. In a skillet heat olive oil and pour the egg mixture
3. Cook for 1-2 minutes per side
4. When ready remove omelette from the skillet and serve

RED ONION OMELETTE

Serves: *1*

Prep Time: *5* Minutes

Cook Time: *10* Minutes

Total Time: *15* Minutes

INGREDIENTS

- 2 eggs
- ¼ tsp salt
- ¼ tsp black pepper
- 1 tablespoon olive oil
- ¼ cup cheese
- ¼ tsp basil
- 1 cup red onion

DIRECTIONS

1. In a bowl combine all ingredients together and mix well
2. In a skillet heat olive oil and pour the egg mixture
3. Cook for 1-2 minutes per side
4. When ready remove omelette from the skillet and serve

TOMATO OMELETTE

Serves: *1*

Prep Time: *5*   Minutes

Cook Time: *10*   Minutes

Total Time: *15*   Minutes

INGREDIENTS

- 2 eggs
- ¼ tsp salt
- ¼ tsp black pepper
- 1 tablespoon olive oil
- ¼ cup cheese
- ¼ tsp basil
- 1 cup tomatoes

DIRECTIONS

1. In a bowl combine all ingredients together and mix well
2. In a skillet heat olive oil and pour the egg mixture
3. Cook for 1-2 minutes per side
4. When ready remove omelette from the skillet and serve

BLUEBERRIES GRANOLA

Serves: **2**

Prep Time: **10** Minutes

Cook Time: **40** Minutes

Total Time: **50** Minutes

INGREDIENTS

- 1 cup blueberries
- 2 cup porridge oats
- 2 oz. coconut flakes
- 2 oz. brown sugar
- 2 tablespoons honey
- 1/2 cup raisins
- 1 cup chocolate chips

DIRECTIONS

1. In a bowl combine all ingredients together and mix well
2. Spread mixture on a baking sheet
3. Bake at 275 F for 30-40 minutes
4. When ready remove from the oven, cut into bars and serve

CARROT CAKE GRANOLA

Serves: **4-6**

Prep Time: **10** Minutes

Cook Time: **40** Minutes

Total Time: **50** Minutes

INGREDIENTS

- 1 cup oats
- 1 tsp mixed spice
- ¼ lb. walnuts
- 2 carrots
- 2 oz. coconut oil
- 2 oz. honey

DIRECTIONS

1. In a bowl combine all ingredients together and mix well
2. Place the mixture into a baking dish
3. Bake at 350 F for 30-40 minutes
4. When ready remove from the oven and serve

CINNAMON GRANOLA BARS

Serves: *6-8*
Prep Time: *10*   Minutes

Cook Time: *40*   Minutes

Total Time: *50*   Minutes

INGREDIENTS

- ¼ lb. butter
- 2 cups oats
- ¼ lb. sunflower seeds
- 2 oz. sesame seeds
- 2 oz. walnuts
- 2 tablespoons honey
- 1 tsp cinnamon
- 1 cup cherries
- 1 cup blueberries

DIRECTIONS

1. In a bowl combine all ingredients together and mix well
2. Place the mixture into a baking dish
3. Bake at 350 F for 30-40 minutes
4. When ready remove from the oven cut into bars and serve

ORANGE GRANOLA

Serves: *6-8*

Prep Time: *10*   Minutes

Cook Time: *35*   Minutes

Total Time: *45*   Minutes

INGREDIENTS

- 1 lb. oats
- Juice from 1 orange
- 1 tsp cinnamon
- 2 oz. almonds
- 2 oz. sunflower seeds

DIRECTIONS

1. Place all ingredients, except orange juice, in a blender and blend until smooth
2. In a saucepan boil the orange juice and mix with the mixture and cook until the liquid has evaporated
3. Spread the mixture on a baking sheet
4. Bake at 350 F for 15-20 minutes
5. When ready remove from the oven cut into bars and serve

FRENCH TOAST

Serves: *4*
Prep Time: *10* Minutes

Cook Time: *20* Minutes

Total Time: *30* Minutes

INGREDIENTS

- 1 tablespoon olive oil
- 4 eggs
- 100 ml double cream
- ¼ tsp cinnamon
- ¼ tsp nutmeg
- ¼ tsp peanut butter
- 4 bread slices

DIRECTIONS

1. In a bowl combine all ingredients together and mix well
2. Place the bread into the dipping and let the bread soak for 3-4 minutes
3. In a skillet heat olive oil and fry the bread for 2-3 minutes per side
4. When ready remove from the skillet and serve

BEANS OMELETTE

Serves: *1*
Prep Time: *5*   Minutes

Cook Time: *10*   Minutes

Total Time: *15*   Minutes

INGREDIENTS

- 2 eggs
- ¼ tsp salt
- ¼ tsp black pepper
- 1 tablespoon olive oil
- ¼ cup cheese
- ¼ tsp basil
- 1 cup beans

DIRECTIONS

1. In a bowl combine all ingredients together and mix well
2. In a skillet heat olive oil and pour the egg mixture
3. Cook for 1-2 minutes per side
4. When ready remove omelette from the skillet and serve

Serves: 2
Prep Time: 5   Minutes

Cook Time: 30   Minutes

Total Time: 35   Minutes

INGREDIENTS

- 1 tsp vanilla extract
- 1 tablespoon honey
- 1 lb. rolled oats
- 2 tablespoons sesame seeds
- ¼ lb. almonds
- ¼ lb. berries

DIRECTIONS

1. Preheat the oven to 325 F
2. Spread the granola onto a baking sheet
3. Bake for 12-15 minutes, remove and mix everything
4. Bake for another 12-15 minutes or until slightly brown
5. When ready remove from the oven and serve

BLUEBERRY PANCAKES

Serves: *4*

Prep Time: *10*   Minutes

Cook Time: *20*   Minutes

Total Time: *30*   Minutes

INGREDIENTS

- 1 cup whole wheat flour
- ¼ tsp baking soda
- ¼ tsp baking powder
- 1 cup blueberries
- 1 cup milk

DIRECTIONS

1. In a bowl combine all ingredients together and mix well
2. In a skillet heat olive oil
3. Pour ¼ of the batter and cook each pancake for 1-2 minutes per side
4. When ready remove from heat and serve

CURRANTS PANCAKES

Serves: **4**

Prep Time: **10** Minutes

Cook Time: **30** Minutes

Total Time: **40** Minutes

INGREDIENTS

- 1 cup whole wheat flour
- ¼ tsp baking soda
- ¼ tsp baking powder
- 1 cup currants
- 1 cup milk

DIRECTIONS

1. In a bowl combine all ingredients together and mix well
2. In a skillet heat olive oil
3. Pour ¼ of the batter and cook each pancake for 1-2 minutes per side
4. When ready remove from heat and serve

COCONUT PANCAKES

Serves: **4**

Prep Time: **10**   Minutes

Cook Time: **20**   Minutes

Total Time: **30**   Minutes

INGREDIENTS

- 1 cup whole wheat flour
- ¼ tsp baking soda
- ¼ tsp baking powder
- ¼ cup coconut flakes
- 1 cup milk

DIRECTIONS

1. In a bowl combine all ingredients together and mix well
2. In a skillet heat olive oil
3. Pour ¼ of the batter and cook each pancake for 1-2 minutes per side
4. When ready remove from heat and serve

WALNUT PANCAKES

Serves: **4**

Prep Time: **10** Minutes

Cook Time: **20** Minutes

Total Time: **30** Minutes

INGREDIENTS

- 1 cup whole wheat flour
- ¼ tsp baking soda
- ¼ tsp baking powder
- 1 cup coconut flakes
- 1 cup milk

DIRECTIONS

1. In a bowl combine all ingredients together and mix well
2. In a skillet heat olive oil
3. Pour ¼ of the batter and cook each pancake for 1-2 minutes per side
4. When ready remove from heat and serve

PANCAKES

Serves: *4*

Prep Time: *10*   Minutes

Cook Time: *30*   Minutes

Total Time: *40*   Minutes

INGREDIENTS

- 1 cup whole wheat flour
- ¼ tsp baking soda
- ¼ tsp baking powder
- 1 cup milk

DIRECTIONS

1. In a bowl combine all ingredients together and mix well
2. In a skillet heat olive oil
3. Pour ¼ of the batter and cook each pancake for 1-2 minutes per side
4. When ready remove from heat and serve

RAISIN BREAKFAST MIX

Serves: *1*
Prep Time: *5*   Minutes

Cook Time: *5*   Minutes

Total Time: *10* Minutes

INGREDIENTS

- ½ cup dried raisins
- ½ cup dried pecans
- ¼ cup almonds
- 1 cup coconut milk
- 1 tsp cinnamon

DIRECTIONS

1. In a bowl combine all ingredients together
2. Serve with milk

SAUSAGE BREAKFAST SANDWICH

Serves: **2**

Prep Time: **5**   Minutes

Cook Time: **15**   Minutes

Total Time: **20**   Minutes

INGREDIENTS

- ¼ cup egg substitute
- 1 muffin
- 1 turkey sausage patty
- 1 tablespoon cheddar cheese

DIRECTIONS

1. In a skillet pour egg and cook on low heat
2. Place turkey sausage patty in a pan and cook for 4-5 minutes per side
3. On a toasted muffin place the cooked egg, top with a sausage patty and cheddar cheese
4. Serve when ready

STRAWBERRY MUFFINS

Serves: **8-12**

Prep Time: **10** Minutes

Cook Time: **20** Minutes

Total Time: **30** Minutes

INGREDIENTS

- 2 eggs
- 1 tablespoon olive oil
- 1 cup milk
- 2 cups whole wheat flour
- 1 tsp baking soda
- ¼ tsp baking soda
- 1 tsp cinnamon
- 1 cup strawberries

DIRECTIONS

1. In a bowl combine all wet ingredients
2. In another bowl combine all dry ingredients
3. Combine wet and dry ingredients together
4. Pour mixture into 8-12 prepared muffin cups, fill 2/3 of the cups
5. Bake for 18-20 minutes at 375 F
6. When ready remove from the oven and serve

DESSERTS

BREAKFAST COOKIES

Serves: *8-12*

Prep Time: 5   Minutes

Cook Time: *15*   Minutes

Total Time: *20*   Minutes

INGREDIENTS

- 1 cup rolled oats
- ¼ cup applesauce
- ½ tsp vanilla extract
- 3 tablespoons chocolate chips
- 2 tablespoons dried fruits
- 1 tsp cinnamon

DIRECTIONS

1. Preheat the oven to 325 F
2. In a bowl combine all ingredients together and mix well
3. Scoop cookies using an ice cream scoop
4. Place cookies onto a prepared baking sheet
5. Place in the oven for 12-15 minutes or until the cookies are done
6. When ready remove from the oven and serve

BLUEBERRY PIE

Serves: *8-12*
Prep Time: *15*   Minutes

Cook Time: *35*   Minutes

Total Time: *50*   Minutes

INGREDIENTS

- pastry sheets
- ¼ tsp lavender
- 1 cup brown sugar
- 4-5 cups blueberries
- 1 tablespoon lemon juice
- 1 cup almonds
- 2 tablespoons butter

DIRECTIONS

1. Line a pie plate or pie form with pastry and cover the edges of the plate depending on your preference
2. In a bowl combine all pie ingredients together and mix well
3. Pour the mixture over the pastry
4. Bake at 400-425 F for 25-30 minutes or until golden brown
5. When ready remove from the oven and let it rest for 15 minutes

PUMPKIN PIE

Serves: *8-12*

Prep Time: *15*   Minutes

Cook Time: *35*   Minutes

Total Time: *50*   Minutes

INGREDIENTS

- pastry sheets
- 1 cup buttermilk
- 1 can pumpkin
- 1 cup sugar
- 1 tsp cinnamon
- 1 tsp vanilla extract
- 2 eggs

DIRECTIONS

1. Line a pie plate or pie form with pastry and cover the edges of the plate depending on your preference
2. In a bowl combine all pie ingredients together and mix well
3. Pour the mixture over the pastry
4. Bake at 400-425 F for 25-30 minutes or until golden brown
5. When ready remove from the oven and let it rest for 15 minutes

RICOTTA ICE-CREAM

Serves: *6-8*

Prep Time: *15*   Minutes
Cook Time: *15*   Minutes
Total Time: *30*   Minutes

INGREDIENTS

- 1 cup almonds
- 1-pint vanilla ice cream
- 2 cups ricotta cheese
- 1 cup honey

DIRECTIONS

1. In a saucepan whisk together all ingredients
2. Mix until bubbly
3. Strain into a bowl and cool
4. Whisk in favorite fruits and mix well
5. Cover and refrigerate for 2-3 hours
6. Pour mixture in the ice-cream maker and follow manufacturer instructions
7. Serve when ready

SAFFRON ICE-CREAM

Serves: **6-8**

Prep Time: **15**   Minutes

Cook Time: **15**   Minutes

Total Time: **30**   Minutes

INGREDIENTS

- 4 egg yolks
- 1 cup heavy cream
- 1 cup milk
- ½ cup brown sugar
- 1 tsp saffron
- 1 tsp vanilla extract

DIRECTIONS

1. In a saucepan whisk together all ingredients
2. Mix until bubbly
3. Strain into a bowl and cool
4. Whisk in favorite fruits and mix well
5. Cover and refrigerate for 2-3 hours
6. Pour mixture in the ice-cream maker and follow manufacturer instructions
7. Serve when ready

FIG SMOOTHIE

Serves: *1*
Prep Time: 5   Minutes

Cook Time: 5   Minutes

Total Time: *10*   Minutes

INGREDIENTS

- 1 cup ice
- 1 cup vanilla yogurt
- 1 cup coconut milk
- 1 tsp honey
- 4 figs

DIRECTIONS

1. In a blender place all ingredients and blend until smooth
2. Pour smoothie in a glass and serve

POMEGRANATE SMOOTHIE

Serves: **1**

Prep Time: **5**   Minutes

Cook Time: **5**   Minutes

Total Time: **10**   Minutes

INGREDIENTS

- 2 cups blueberries
- 1 cup pomegranate
- 1 tablespoon honey
- 1 cup Greek yogurt

DIRECTIONS

1. In a blender place all ingredients and blend until smooth
2. Pour smoothie in a glass and serve

Serves: *1*
Prep Time: 5   Minutes

Cook Time: 5   Minutes

Total Time: *10*   Minutes

INGREDIENTS

- 1 cup kale
- 1 banana
- 1 cup almond milk
- 1 cup vanilla yogurt
- 1 tsp chia seeds
- ¼ tsp ginger

DIRECTIONS

1. In a blender place all ingredients and blend until smooth
2. Pour smoothie in a glass and serve

BERRY YOGHURT SMOOTHIE

Serves: *1*

Prep Time: *5*   Minutes

Cook Time: *5*   Minutes

Total Time: *10*   Minutes

INGREDIENTS

- 6 oz. berries
- 2 bananas
- 4 oz. vanilla yoghurt
- 1 cup milk
- 1 tablespoon honey

DIRECTIONS

1. In a blender place all ingredients and blend until smooth
2. Pour smoothie in a glass and serve

COCONUT SMOOTHIE

Serves: *1*
Prep Time: *5*   Minutes

Cook Time: *5*   Minutes

Total Time: *10*   Minutes

INGREDIENTS

- 2 mangoes
- 2 bananas
- 1 cup coconut water
- 1 cup ice
- 1 tablespoon honey
- 1 cup Greek Yoghurt
- 1 cup strawberries

DIRECTIONS

1. In a blender place all ingredients and blend until smooth
2. Pour smoothie in a glass and serve

RASPBERRY-VANILLA SMOOTHIE

Serves: **1**

Prep Time: **5**   Minutes

Cook Time: **5**   Minutes

Total Time: **10** Minutes

INGREDIENTS

- ¼ cup sugar
- ¼ cup water
- 1 cup Greek yoghurt
- 1 cup raspberries
- 1 tsp vanilla extract
- 1 cup ice

DIRECTIONS

1. In a blender place all ingredients and blend until smooth
2. Pour smoothie in a glass and serve

CHERRY SMOOTHIE

Serves: *1*

Prep Time: 5   Minutes

Cook Time: 5   Minutes

Total Time: *10*   Minutes

INGREDIENTS

- 1 can cherries
- 2 tablespoons peanut butter
- 1 tablespoon honey
- 1 cup Greek Yoghurt
- 1 cup coconut milk

DIRECTIONS

1. In a blender place all ingredients and blend until smooth
2. Pour smoothie in a glass and serve

CHOCOLATE SMOOTHIE

Serves: **1**

Prep Time: **5**   Minutes

Cook Time: **5**   Minutes

Total Time: **10**   Minutes

INGREDIENTS

- 2 bananas
- 1 cup Greek Yoghurt
- 1 tablespoon honey
- 1 tablespoon cocoa powder
- ½ cup chocolate chips
- ¼ cup almond milk

DIRECTIONS

1. In a blender place all ingredients and blend until smooth
2. Pour smoothie in a glass and serve

TOFU SMOOTHIE

Serves: *1*
Prep Time: *5*   Minutes

Cook Time: *5*   Minutes

Total Time: *10* Minutes

INGREDIENTS

- 1 cup blueberries
- ¼ cup tofu
- ¼ cup pomegranate juice
- 1 cup ice
- ½ cup agave nectar

DIRECTIONS

1. In a blender place all ingredients and blend until smooth
2. Pour smoothie in a glass and serve

ORANGE SMOOTHIE

Serves: *1*

Prep Time: *5*   Minutes

Cook Time: *5*   Minutes

Total Time: *10*   Minutes

INGREDIENTS

- 1 orange
- ½ cup orange juice
- ½ banana
- 1 tsp vanilla essence

DIRECTIONS

1. In a blender place all ingredients and blend until smooth
2. Pour smoothie in a glass and serve

Serves: *1*

Prep Time: 5   Minutes

Cook Time: 5   Minutes

Total Time: *10*   Minutes

INGREDIENTS

- ¼ cup raisins
- 2 Medjool dates
- 1 cup berries
- 1 cup almond milk
- 1 tsp chia seeds

DIRECTIONS

1. In a blender place all ingredients and blend until smooth
2. Pour smoothie in a glass and serve

CPSIA information can be obtained
at www.ICGtesting.com
Printed in the USA
BVHW031011150321
602551BV00004B/207